A SIMPLE MEMOIR OF MY EARLY YEARS

FOR MY GRANDCHILDREN

IN MY OWN WORDS

GERTRUD JACKLE

A Simple Memoir of My Early Years

Gertrud Jackle

Copyright © 2019 Gertrud Jackle

Published by 1st World Publishing
P.O. Box 2211, Fairfield, Iowa 52556
tel: 641-209-5000 • fax: 866-440-5234
web: www.1stworldpublishing.com

First Edition

LCCN: 2019933433

Softcover ISBN: 978-1-4218-3621-8

Hardcover ISBN: 978-1-4218-3622-5

All rights reserved. No part of this book may be reproduced or utilized in any form or by any means, electronic or mechanical, including photocopying or recording, or by any information storage and retrieval system, without permission in writing from the author.

This material has been written and published for educational purposes to enhance one's well-being. In regard to health issues, the information is not intended as a substitute for appropriate care and advice from health professionals, nor does it equate to the assumption of medical or any other form of liability on the part of the publisher or author. The publisher and author shall have neither liability nor responsibility to any person or entity with respect to loss, damages, or injury claimed to be caused directly or indirectly by any information in this book.

Dedicated to My Grandchildren

Drew Baldock

Lindsay Baldock

Anya Charles

Amman Charles

Old Testament
Corinthians 13 - 4 - 7

Love is patient, Love is kind.
it does not envy, it does not boast,
it is not proud.
It does not dishonor others, it is not self seeking
it is not easly angered, it keeps not record of wrongs
Love does not delight in evil but rejoices with the truth
it always protects always trusts, always hopes,
always perseveres.

G Jackee
May 20 2019

FOREWORD

For Drew, Lindsay, Anya, and Amman.

This simple memoir is a modest attempt to share the early accounts of your grandmother, Gertrud Jackle (Stoltz), with her four grandchildren. Hopefully, it will spur you to capture a glimpse of her early challenges—which are so unlike your own experience growing up today.

The information is largely anecdotal, predominantly from your grandmother's memories—recollections stirred by revisiting personal black and white photos taken during the first twenty years of her family life. Her brother, Julian, also contributed his memories to fill in the understandably large gaps of the early years of the Stolz family.

Your grandmother was a young child growing up in war-torn turmoil prior to and during World War II. It was challenging to place her memories within the context of history; however, this brief record details a few layers of her background and notable experiences as narrated in her own simple words. Some dates may be slightly unreliable, but nonetheless, they illustrate her initial intentions.

It's useful to remember that most of these events occurred more than half a century before you were born and are, in direct ways, integral to your own growth, development, and character.

Erika Jackle
September 21, 2017

A NOTE ABOUT PHOTOGRAPHS

In the 'olden days,' most people didn't own personal cameras, especially during wartimes in Europe. Most photos were taken by a hired professional who owned a single camera, often the size of a small shoe box. How Mom was able to acquire and retain these images in the midst of losing everything, fleeing armies, and immigrating across the Atlantic is a mystery onto itself.

Also, we invite you to view an impromptu YouTube video of your Oma chatting a little bit about the stories included in this collection. Trying to remember your childhood is difficult for anyone, but all the more so when you are eighty-five years old.

Search YouTube: Gertrud Jackle, A Simple Memoir of My Early Years.

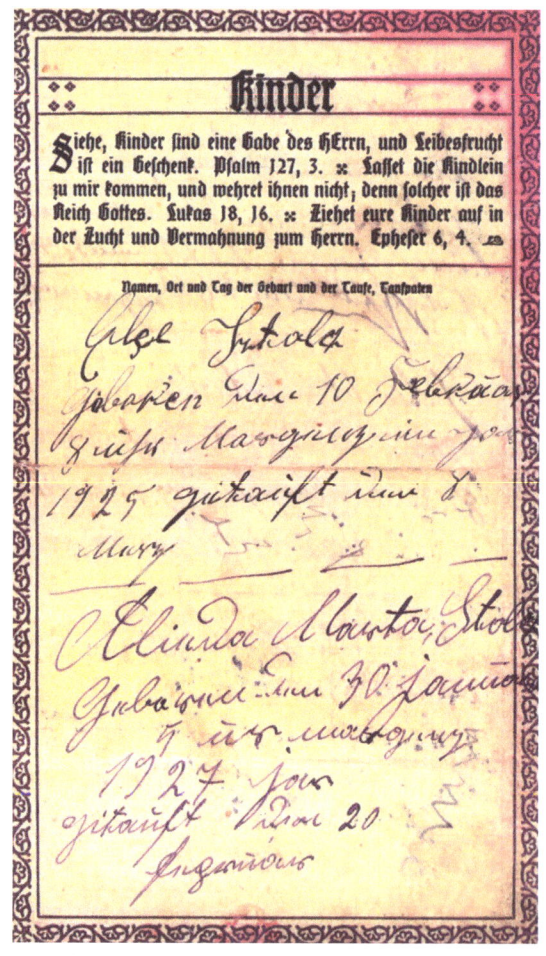 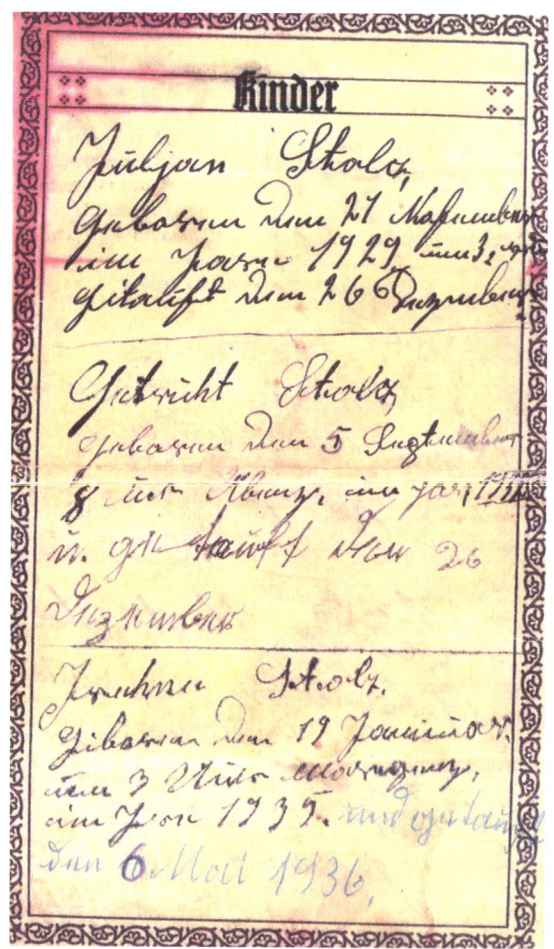

First pages of the Stoltz family bible with birth dates. It was a common practice to record birthdays in the family bible.

STOLTZ FAMILY TREE

Maternal Great-Great Grandfather: Michael Wolter
Born: 1812 Lipia Gora, Poland
Died: Mar., 14, 1890 Osowiec, Masovian Poland
↓

Maternal Great-Great Grandmother: Karoline Benkendorf
Born: 1814 Pasieka, Poland
Died: Feb. 21, 1886 Lorbiork (Lebork?), Poland
↓

Paternal Great Grandparents:
Great Grandfather: Friedrich Stoltz
Great Grandmother: Anna Spitzer
↓

Maternal Great Grandparents:
Great Grandfather: Karl Hertel
Great Grandmother: Rosin Glaser
↓

Paternal Grandfather: Gottlieb Stoltz
Born: Oct. 28, 1860 Nowy, Soviet Poland
Died: May 6, 1936 Schischinskie Holendry, Poland
farmer
↓

Maternal Grandfather: Paul Schrank
Born: May 24, 1857 Zonski, Poland
Died: Aug. 21 1941 Zonski, Poland
farmer
↓

Paternal Grandmother: Mathilde Hertel
Born: 1862 Chartow, Poland
Died: Dec. 11, 1930 Schischinskie Holendry, Poland
housewife
↓

Maternal Grandmother: Mathilde Wolter
Born: Oct. 13, 1855 Lesiska, Poland
Died: July 12, 1924 Lesiska, Poland
housewife
↓

Father: Wilhelm Stoltz
Born: Jan. 21, 1891 Zapfener Hauland, Poland
Died: Oct. 21, 1936 Zapfener Hauland, Poland
Occupation: farmer, married in Sompolno Jan. 27, 1924 (Evengelical)

Mother: Berta Stoltz nee Schrank
Born: May 28, 1893 Laczki, Poland
Died: Mar. 5, 1938 Zapfener Hauland, Poland

Children: all born in Schischinskie Holendry, Zapfener Hauland, in German Poland
  Else: Born Feb. 10, 1925   Died
  Alita: Born Jan. 30, 1927
  Julian: Born Nov. 21, 1929
  Gertrud: Born Sept. 5, 1932
  Irene: Born Jan. 19, 1935

Distant ancestors: Christian Wolter, Erna Disterhoft, Gottfried Benkendorf, Ludwika Besler (emigrated to Poland from Germany, possibly from near the Eifel mountain range in western Germany.

   The Eifel is a low mountain range in western Germany and eastern Belgium. It occupies parts of southwestern North Rhine-Westphalia, northwestern Rhineland-Palatinate and the south of the German-speaking Community of Belgium.).

Me at Wascana Park, 1953.

TABLE OF CONTENTS

Foreword 5
Family Tree 7
Parents and Early Childhood Memories 11
Wartime Memories 26
Fleeing Poland 30
Evacuation 32
Life After the War 36
Living in Canada 45
How I Want to Be Remembered 61
Index of Photographs 63
Footnotes 76

PARENTS AND EARLY CHILDHOOD MEMORIES

I know very little about my grandparents. What I do know was conveyed to me by my brother, Julian.

Grandfather Shrank, my grandfather on mom's side, was a farmer and carpenter who built spinning wheels.

Grandfather Stoltz, my grandfather on dad's side, was a farmer and gristmill (a mill for grinding grain) operator.

We were a German family. Regardless of the fact that our family had been born in Poland for generations, we were considered German. Everyone's passport said 'German'. There was only one Polish family in the region where we lived and all of the Germans were Lutheran and religion was taught in our schools.

My father's name was Wilhelm Stoltz. He was born on January 21, 1891, in Zapfener Hauland, a district in Poland. He had 3 brothers, Julius, August, and Bruno, and 4 sisters, Martha, Augusta (twin to August), Bertha, and Julia.

There were eight children in his family. In order from oldest to youngest: Martha (Kitzman), Julius, Wilhelm (my dad), twins Augusta (Schulberg) and August, Bertha (Fritz), Julia (Kelm), and Bruno. I have only one picture of my father and a few of his family.

(Wilhelm Stoltz. This is the only existing photo of my father. It was cropped from a photo taken with his brother (presumably Julius) in Chicago when he immigrated to the USA in approximately 1912.)

My father immigrated to the USA with his older brother, Julius Stoltz, and two sisters, Bertha and Martha, in approximately 1912, as I recall. He and Martha returned to Poland in 1913.

Before leaving for Chicago, my father had purchased additional land for the family farm. We believe it must have been his intention to return from the USA to take over the farm, but we are not sure why he went through the immigration process in the first place. Later, Martha returned to live in Chicago permanently.

(Poland was divided into three partitions prior to World War I: Russian, German, and Austria-Hungary. While Poland did not exist as an independent state during World War I, its geographical position between the fighting powers meant that much fighting and terrific human and material losses occurred on the Polish lands between 1914 and 1918.

This circumstance afforded the Poles political leverage as both sides offered pledges of concessions and future autonomy in exchange for Polish loyalty and army recruits.

The Austrians wanted to incorporate Russian territory into their territory, so even before the war, they allowed nationalist organizations to form there.)

My brother, Julian, told us that our dad was his mother's pet and while he was enlisted, she would send him personal items. Unfortunately, these shipments were frequently intercepted by the officers who would pilfer them for themselves.

Once war broke out, she lost contact with him. He was not seen or heard from for seven years—three years after WW1 ended.

We were told he was severely injured in the war by the Germans, but the Russian Revolution which overthrew the tsarist regime took place in March and November of 1917, so he could easily have been caught up and injured in that uprising.

His mother alleged that once the revolution started, the soldiers turned against the officers and our dad threw one of the officers in the Volga River.

Injured on the battlefield, he lay there for 3 days before he was found. He survived on half-ripe apples until he was discovered and taken to a hospital in Crimea to recover.

His body was severely damaged by shrapnel on one side. His injuries left him with one lung, damage to his stomach, missing ribs, and a badly injured knee. He had a metal plate implanted on his injured chest to support the shattered side of his wounded body.

For seven years, no one knew if he was dead or alive. The account claims he was living with a Russian baroness during this time. Julian speculates we may have half cousins from this relationship.

Augusta was still living on the farm when her brother finally returned to Poland and the events of his wartime involvement came through her to Julian.

He was severely disabled by his injuries and was given a pension. She remembers him continuing to smoke cigarettes, and when he did so, smoke would exit from the metal plates of his injured chest.

She remembers he was very outspoken after the war and it was felt he was deeply "red" or socialist in his political beliefs. Family members were concerned about this as there was fear that Russian socialism would appropriate everything they had worked for.

I was very young, so I don't remember much about this time, but I somehow remember that my uncle Julius was a tanner. He married an Italian woman and became a manager at a tannery. His younger son, Clarence, was tall like my grandson Drew.

Martha Kitzman and Julius eventually settled in Chicago. Many years later, Martha sent winter clothing to us when we emigrated to Canada.

Aunt (Augusta) Schulberg Immigrated to Canada and settled in Yorkton, Saskatchewan, where she bought a small farm. Years later, she relocated to Victoria, British Columbia. I kept in contact with her until she died in 1987.

August was a chronic alcoholic. His wife was reclusive and rarely seen. She didn't even attend my mother's funeral. When August's wife died, he was in the army and was not allowed to return home for the funeral because his drinking was so unwarranted and excessive, he was deemed unfit. His son was sent home to take care of funeral matters.

Julian says that our father, Wilhelm, had invested money into the family farm with an additional land purchase. With the death of his father, (my grandfather) the brothers were paid out their share based on the value of the land their dad owned. August felt cheated and thought he was due more money for his share of the estate.

We are not sure how he died, but we suspect he died from his addiction. He died in Poland, but I am not sure of the date. More on him later.

Julia Kelm settled in Windsor, Ontario.
Bruno settled in New Westminster, British Columbia in 1929.
Bertha immigrated to Canada and ended up in Ontario.

Aunt Schulberg on her Yorkton farm—late 1950s or early 1960s.

Aunt Augusta Schulberg at our wedding in September 1953.

Aunt Schulberg and I in Victoria, Canada—1986.

My father met my mother, Berta Schrank (born May 28, 1893, in Laczki, Poland), after THE GREAT WAR (WW1), and they married in an evangelical church at Sompolno, Poland on January 27, 1924. He was 33; she was 30. They had 5 children together: Else on February 10, 1925; Alita (Ali) on January 30, 1927; Julian on November 21, 1929; me, Gertrud, on September 4, 1932; and Irene on January 19, 1935. We were all born in Schischinskie Holendry, Zapfener Hauland, in German Poland where the family farm was located.

It was a small farm, about 40 European acres, which is 80 acres in North America. It was separated into 2 parts by a highway and was involved in mixed farming. We had dairy cows, hogs, grain crops, and sugar beets crops on contract to a factory which processed the beets into sugar and syrup.

My brother remembers two black horses which he and Ali rode whenever they had an opportunity. They rode bareback with no bridle or harness until they fell off.

The only memory I have of my father is a story I was told about how he died while shaking a plum tree. He was attempting to get all the fruit to fall, but his overexertion caused a hemorrhage in his remaining lung. He was 45 years old when he died on October 21, 1936.

I remember my mother was very ill with what was probably tuberculosis—and Else, being the eldest, still a child herself, looked after us. My mother died on March 5, 1938, at the age of 43 shortly after the death of my father, Wilhelm. This left us as orphans, ranging in age from 3 to 13 years old. I was just five years old. There was no possibility of any one family member taking all of us in, so the five of us were split up and stayed with respective family members within Poland.

Left to right: Ali, Julian, Else, Gertrud, Aunt Lück, Irene. Aunt Lück is my mother's sister. I have no clear memory of her..

My mother's funeral. We five children were split up and were cared for by some of the adults in this photograph.
Back row L-R: Uncle Litwitz (married to my mom's sister); Uncle Shrank (my mom's oldest brother); Aunt Shrank (wife to Uncle Shrank): cousin Schmidt (on mom's side); wife to my nephew (on right); my nephew (son to mom's oldest sister)
Middle Row L- R: Uncle August Stoltz (my mom's youngest brother): Aunt Litwitz (my mom's sister); unidentified woman; probably cousin Lonya Litwitz (eldest of 3 Litwitz daughters); Aunt Amelia Schmidt; (my mom's sister); Aunt Schmidt (married to Uncle Schmidt above her); Aunt Lück (mom's sister); my aunt (mom's oldest sister); my uncle (married to mom's oldest sister)
Front Row L-R: Uncle Lück (married to mom's sister); my cousin (a Lück daughter); unidentified man; my cousin, (a Lück daughter); my eldest sister Else; my sister Ali; my brother Julian; me, Gertrud; my youngest sister Irene; possibly my cousin, the eldest Litwitz daughter

My mother was one of 8 children. She had two brothers, but one Shrank brother died. Her youngest, Amelia, married a Litwitz and it was Aunt Amelia Litwitz who took me in when my mother died.

There is an interesting story about our mother's death. Evidently, she kept her father's gold watch locked in a small drawer in her kitchen table. August (my father's brother) stole the watch and she was so stunned and traumatized by this incident that she collapsed on the spot, never spoke again, and took to her bed where she died days or weeks later. Julian thought she had a cold which developed into pneumonia and the trauma of the theft incident with August contributed to her demise.

There are no photos of my mom while she was living, but Julian says she looks most like her sister, Amelia Litwitz, in the funeral photo.

Another story I was told occurred when I was a young toddler, still unable to talk. Apparently, I wandered far away from the farm, down a gravel road to the next town, Slesin, where a local family picked me up on the road and took me to their home. I was missing for three days. Somehow, news reached them about a missing child, and I was taken to a nearby town and eventually home. I'm very fortunate that nothing ill-fated happened to me that day.

Following the death of my mother, we all depended on our Aunts and Uncles for our survival. Uncle Shrank (brother to my mom's dad) assumed control of the farm and the children, as he was the oldest son. He had 12 children of his own and Julian believed he was good at "breeding" but not at running a farm. Uncle Shrank hired a farmer to manage the farm, and using the rent revenue from the farm, paid the relatives to look after the five children. Neither Uncle Shrank or the renter-farmer did a very good job of management. At some point Uncle Krueger took over being executor of the estate. Julian thinks Uncle Shrank was more than happy to give up his responsibilities.

When Uncle Krueger took over, he got rid of the renter-farmer, hired another, better one, and opened bank accounts for each of the children. He thought it was shameful that these family guardians were working the orphan children so hard and getting paid for it.

Uncle Krueger was responsible for the payouts to the guardians. He was a cousin to my dad and executor to the family estate/farm. He and his wife had no children of their own. He was an exceptional manager of the farm, was mayor and county reeve of Wolfsburg (a fair-sized town that survived the war and still exists today), was once the fire chief, and had close connections to the police chief and the head of the draft department.

My Uncle Krueger with his niece and her child, 1943

My brother, Julian, remembers that he and Ali were a little wild (very active, high energy, independent spirits) and nobody wanted them. I don't know if this was the case or not, but I do know that they have always been this way, and this could be perceived as being hard to handle when they were children.

Else lived with Uncle Litwitz initially, but later worked for a family cousin for room and board who was a school teacher and preacher. She developed tuberculosis during the time she spent in the refugee camp after the Russian evacuation. It is here that she met her future husband, Harry, and an elderly lady, Hilda, who lived with her after the war. She was known to all of us as Aunt Hilda. Else was treated in a sanatorium, probably near Holstein prior to her marriage to Harry.

Else visited me from time to time. It was during the period that Hitler invaded Poland, but before we fled for Germany. She kept track of where every member of the family was located and would occasionally take me along to visit my youngest sister, Irene.

My oldest sister, Else.

My youngest sister, Irene. I believe this is her confirmation photo. 1948.

Irene was initially intended to be placed with Aunt Lück in the village, but Aunt Lück had many children of her own, so Uncle August was chosen to be her guardian. Unfortunately, Uncle August abused Irene's estate dividend and spent the money on alcohol.

When Irene's money was no longer sent to Uncle August, he took baby Irene to Uncle Shrank's and left her on a pillow in front of the farmhouse. He never said anything to anyone, just left her there and took off. It is unclear what August's wife's involvement in this decision was. It probably didn't help that Irene had health issues.

Irene had a disability which left her partially unable to use her right arm and hand. Whether because of her disability, which wasn't understood at the time, or because she was not immediate family, Irene was mistreated by her foster family. She was made to eat in the corner and not with the family. She was the last one to be looked after. She had very curly hair and cried when it was brushed.

Else visited Uncle August a couple of times and brought gifts for Irene. She said they would pick Irene up when she arrived and put her down as soon as she left. She felt she was not properly cared for. Initially, we thought Irene's physical disabilities (which began at age three) were due to polio, but it was later discovered that she had a tumor on her brain.

So, Uncle Shrank and his wife now have 13 children, including Irene with her disability. They looked after her until after the war. Julian was able to track down Aunt Shrank and learned that Uncle Shrank had been killed by the Polish people in the village who hated the Germans. He died a brutal death when the people put a door on him and stomped him to death.

Irene was separated from the family during the evacuation of Poland. Many years later, after the war, she was found in a Catholic orphanage by the Red Cross. Once found, she was placed in another government-funded home where medical testing determined she had a brain tumor. She received treatment and surgery on her disabled arm and leg to improve their function.

When she was initially located after the war, she didn't speak to anyone. It took quite some time for her to feel comfortable enough to start speaking again. She may have been traumatized by being taken from the orphanage with no understanding of who she was, who these people were who claimed to be family and the uncertainty of what was happening to her. It is true that Else taught her to read and write, but Julian confirmed that Irene taught herself measurably, once she was given some basics. She wasn't even able to write her name until Else and Harry took guardianship of her.

Ali, my second oldest sister, was taken in by Uncle Krueger (really a cousin on my dad's side). He was the trustee of the family farm, which he rented out to a Polish family. She was well cared for and got everything she wanted. Uncle Kruger was even willing to pay for her university education. He wanted to set her up with a nephew of his, but she wasn't interested and decided to branch out on her own. We are not sure when Ali left Uncle Krueger's.

Ali still understands a lot of Polish because she went to school in Poland before the war broke out. After the war, Ali acquired a good education in Germany.

Ali and I in Berlin, summer 1950.

My brother, Julian, on the family farm post-war, Poland, 1948.

My brother, Julian, May 1950 in Berlin.

My only brother, Julian, was given to live with Uncle Schmidt, who was married to our mother's oldest sister. He lived there from the age of eight-and-a-half to about ten. He left on his own accord to live with Uncle Litwitz because he knew from a visiting trip with Uncle Schmidt that Else was living there. Unfortunately, by the time he moved there, Else was already gone, boarding with a local family.

Julian, seldom one to complain, mentioned he was frequently beaten by Uncle Litwitz. He supposed Uncle Litwitz may have taken his anger out on him because he had lost a young son in an accident. While picking and loading rocks onto a horse-driven wagon, the wagon rolled over and crushed his son.

Uncle Litwitz had 3 daughters as well, one older, one younger, and one the same age as Julian.

By the time Julian reached fourteen years of age, he had had enough of the beatings and abuse and he wanted control of his life. Else was no longer living there with Uncle Litwitz, so he had every good reason to move on.

Julian tells a story about how Uncle Litwitz wanted to give him another licking for something he didn't deserve. Uncle Litwitz asked him, "Do you want your licking, or do you have a place to go?" Julian replied that he had a place to go, knowing that Uncle Krueger had once told him that if he ever needed a place to go, he could stay there. Uncle Litwitz later apologized, but Julian had a good protector in Uncle Krueger.

Another amusing story Julian recalls is how Uncle Litwitz told him never to smoke. But when the government dispatched cigarettes rations to citizen families, Uncle Litwitz, previously a non-smoker, smoked his own rations, his wife's rations, Julian's rations, and his oldest daughter's rations. He did catch Julian smoking once when he hid a lit cigarette in a wheelbarrow handle. His uncle smoked it as well and didn't say a thing. (Yes, during wartimes, cigarettes were issued to children).

So, Julian left for his family village and stayed with Uncle and Aunt Krueger and Ali from the age of fourteen to twenty-one. At some point, Julian was given his marching orders by the Nazi regime, but those orders were later canceled without explanation. Julian thinks Uncle Krueger's influence and connections kept him from being involuntarily recruited into the regime. On January 29, 1945, the war over, the entire family and village were rounded up and removed to a Russian refugee camp at the Polish/Soviet border which was formerly a barracks for the Russian army. Julian said they were considered prisoners of war. The war was over but the part of Germany, where the camp was located, was now controlled by communist Russia. At some point they stopped calling them POWs (prisoners of war) and started calling them civilians. Nonetheless, no-one was allowed to leave the country or move around freely until April 29, 1950 which was 5 years after they were taken to the camp.

According to Wikipedia, Allies of the German countries were obliged to provide resources, and forced labor as reparation after World War II, in accord with the Potsdam conference held between July 17 and August 2, 1945. Germany was to pay the Allies US$23 billion mainly in machinery and manufacturing plants. Reparations to the Soviet Union stopped in 1953.

This explains how and why Julian and Ali had to work without pay and were unable to leave the country or move around freely. They were the forced labor.

"They were only in the camp a few days before Julian was taken from the camp by a rental farmer to work on his farm."

Apparently local citizens were able to pay the government to use people from the camp for labor. Of course, the prisoners received no payment for their work. Ali was selected to work for a policeman and his family as a domestic in Kónig, but Julian doesn't remember how long she originally remained in the camp. Uncle Krueger must have also been taken to work somewhere, but Julian doesn't know where. A forest ranger enticed Julian to come work for him in the Wollfberg area. Although he was told leaving his present farming position could mean trouble for him, the forest ranger used his connections with the mayor and made the arrangements for Julian to work for him. Some of the people were eventually shipped out by the Russians, and Julian thinks this is how Ali and Uncle Krueger got out.

Photos of Julian in Achon Mines, Germany

Julian had many different jobs, moved around a lot, and never seemed to be without a job for long. These photos are taken at a coal mine in Achon, Germany, on the Dutch border, where he worked for a short time at the age of 22. He is in work clothes on the right. His face is black from coal.

Shortly before he immigrated to Canada, Julian worked for the French Army in Hahn, "Germany Rebuilding". Hahn military airport is now the overflow civilian airport for Frankfurt.

Julian immigrated to Canada on October 27, 1953, two years after me. He first came to Regina, Saskatchewan shortly after my husband, Karl, and I were married. He moved around a lot:

♦ stayed in Regina for a few months with Karl and I in the fall of 1953 while working for the Coop Creamery.

♦ then moved to the Schulberg farm in Yorkton for the winter and spring of 1954. He helped out with chores and construction as they were building a house.

♦ in May of 1954 he traveled to the Yukon where he was employed in seasonal work for the Yukon Consolidated Gold Company until mid-winter, "stripping for the dredge", which is a process which washes down top soil to gravel. He also "towed the dredge", a process that allows you to extract gold using water and mechanical methods. Julian later gave me, and my daughter Erika, jewelry made from gold nuggets and black diamonds from these mines.

♦ traveled to New Westminister, (British Columbia) and boarded on and off with Uncle Bruno; also worked in Kitimat, BC and North Woody with an aluminum company.

♦ enlisted in the Canadian army in Vancouver for a 3-year period (October 1956 – December 1959) with the Princess Patricia's Canadian Light Infantry; received basic airborne training (jumping from planes), and mechanical training in Edmonton; stationed in Calgary, Edmonton and Wainwright.

♦ returned to BC but didn't find work. Moved back to the Yukon (1960) for a short time to work on maintaining the railway bed from Whitehorse to Skagway; then back to Regina briefly.

♦ moved to Kamloops in 1961 for 6 years and worked on the Booth ranch as a cowboy. During the summer holidays from school, my children Erika and Rodney would visit Julian and live on the ranch. This is also where he met and married Edna.

♦ bought his own land in Alberta, May 1966, and became a cattle rancher. He shared time living in Edmonton where he worked with Burns, and gradually built up his cattle business. Sold ranch in 1997.

I was taken in by my Tante Amelia Schmidt, who was my mother's youngest sister. Tante Amelia had 3 sons and a daughter. We lived on a farm in Ludikowo which her eldest son, Erich, looked after. Aunt Amelia was already pensioned off at the time and lived in part of her family home where she could do her own cooking and look after herself. I lived with her, and Erich, his wife (Analiese), and their two children lived in a separate part of the house.

Arthur was Tante Amelia's youngest son. He was living with her at the time I was brought to live in her house. Arthur was injured fighting in the war and was not yet married. A few decades later, Arthur and his grandson, Merko, visited me in Canada. We were living at 2224 Elphinstone Street in Regina at that time. Today, Arthur lives in Germany.

Gustov was Tante Amelia's second son. He was married but had no children. Tante Amelia's daughter, Erna (Bloch), was also married. She lived in East Berlin, which was occupied by Russia, until the war was over. She had quite a few children.

Once the war began, all of Tante Amelia's sons went to war, and only my aunt, her daughter-in-law and her children, and I were left to look after the farm. Unfortunately, Arthur was her only son who survived the war.

During the 1970s, I went to visit my aunt Amelia, who was living with her daughter, Erna, in East Berlin. This was before the Iron Wall came down in 1989. I clearly remember the feeling of being treated like a criminal by the communist authorities.

Tante Amelia with her daughter Erna Bloch after the war in 1944

Post-war photo of Tante Amelia wearing a dress that I sent her from Canada

WARTIME MEMORIES

Sometime before Hitler entered Poland, the Slovaks (we called them the Partisans) attacked our village. Some of my worst memories occurred during this period of my life.

(The Slovak invasion of Poland occurred during Germany's invasion of Poland in 1939. The recently created Slovak Republic joined the attack, and the Slovak Field Army contributed over 50,000 soldiers in three divisions. As the main body of the Polish Home Army forces were engaged with the German armies farther north of the southern border, the Slovak invasion met only weak resistance and suffered minimal losses.
The Polish Resistance Movement, with the Polish Home Army at its forefront, was the largest underground resistance movement in all of occupied Europe, covering both German and Soviet zones of occupied Poland. The Polish resistance is most notable for saving more Jewish lives in the Holocaust than any other Western alliance.
The war began Sept. 1, 1939, with Germany invading Poland from the north, west, and south. The battle ended on Oct. 6, 1939 with Germany and Russia controlling Poland.)

I particularly remember a night when the village dogs started barking loudly, broadcasting the arrival of the Partisan militia. The soldiers treated us badly and tried to extract information from the children by lining us up as in a firing squad and threatening to shoot us if we didn't give them information. I have unfortunate memories of women and children being lined up firing-squad style and threatened with death. I think they wanted information about where the men were hiding—as there were no men around.

A lot of Germans were killed. My aunt told me about a mass grave where many Germans killed by the Slovaks were buried. During this period, while I was living with my Tante Amelia in the village of Ludwikowo in Wartikau province, I started school. I remember my classes being taught in Polish.

I didn't like my Polish teacher and remember having to stand in the corner a lot. My schooling changed to German once the German army occupied our part of Poland. I would have been in school for 5 years until the war ended.

This photo is dated 1942, Poland. I would have been 10 years old. I believe this is my school photo during the German occupation of Poland. I am in the first row, third from the left.

School photo, Children's Home, 1946.

I remember being a tomboy as a child. I particularly liked to climb trees. I injured myself many times and still have the scars on my right arm the day I fell from the loft of a barn.

At home at my aunt Amelia's house, all the children bullied me because I wasn't immediate family. I learned to keep to myself and became even more independent than I was already.

FLEEING POLAND

Nearing the end of the war in the winter of 1944, the Russians were advancing into Poland against the Nazis. Everyone tried to flee across the border into Germany. Aunt Amelia's sons were all at war, resisting the Nazis, so my aunt, her daughter-in-law Anneliese and her children, and I traveled alone. It was wintertime.

As we were fleeing, we loaded horses and buggies and what little we could carry, but the Russians caught up with us and took our horses so they could have fresh horses. We were forced to return to the farm in the village, on foot, with as much as we could carry in our arms. I remember the soldiers hurting the women. They were probably being raped. Some of the women walking with us were pregnant. It must have been a difficult journey for them.

While we were returning back to the farm, we ended up sharing a house with Russian soldiers. These were houses that were evacuated by some of the German people who left Poland. I remember some of the soldiers grabbing me, forcing me back into their room where they were celebrating. Thank God a Russian officer saw this and stopped them. I was fortunate to escape being assaulted by Russian soldiers because of his intervention.

There must have been food left behind in the house because the soldiers were preparing food alongside of us.

We stayed there one or two nights and, fortunately, stayed warm.

When we continued our return to the village, we saw dead people and soldiers frozen on the road. I remember many people were taking boots off the dead bodies to wear them themselves. My feet were freezing and frostbitten, but I couldn't wear those boots.

Just where we were walking, bullets kept flying across the road as the battle continued between the Russians and the Germans. We had to lie flat in the forest to escape the bullets. I remember the whistling sound of the bullets moving through the air.

We were mostly women, children, and old men, as the young men were all at war.

By the time we reached my aunt's farm in Ludikowo, it had been taken over by the Polish people. The farms were originally Polish territory until the Nazis invaded and claimed the land for Nazi Germany, so the Polish hated us because we were German.

We were allowed to stay, but we were expected to work hard.

My aunt's daughter-in-law had to work as a maid for a Polish family, and my job was to look after the cows in the field for a neighboring family. I was to watch over the cows and keep them from straying away. I also had to help look after the younger children in the family. Throughout this time, I was not attending school, and consequently, I lost a year of school.

I remember well the day I fell into the cow's drinking dugout and got stuck. I was cold and alone and afraid that no one would find me, but everything turned out okay. After a while, I was able to pull myself out to safety.

I personally wasn't treated badly by the Polish people, nor was my aunt, but my aunt's daughter-in-law was very disrespectful to the Polish and was therefore treated with disrespect.

One thing I remember well is being chased by boys. I was about eleven years old and was always being chased by older boys. I didn't know what they were going to do with me, but my aunt said to run away from them. She knew I was at risk of being raped.

I also remember lice were very common. Frequently, it got into the sheets of our beds. I was so itchy. Lice were very common at that time. Soldiers had lice from sleeping in the trenches or the hay. This is why it was a common practice for people to boil their sheets and clothing frequently.

Nazi Germany - Third Reich - Forced resettlement of Poland
By Bundesarchiv, R 49 Bild-0138 / Holtfreter, Wilhelm / CC-BY-SA 3.0

Marching to the trains:
Photo credit: By Bundesarchiv, R 49 Bild-0131 / Wilhelm Holtfreter / CC-BY-SA 3.0

EVACUATION

Because it was winter when we first tried to flee Russian occupation and winter again when we were ordered to be evacuated by train cars to Germany, this meant I lost a complete year of school. It was still Russian-occupied Poland when we were forced out, but the Polish families wanted the Germans to stay and work. Nonetheless, all German women, children, and elderly had to leave.

We were kept in an immigration camp while our evacuation papers were being processed. After some time, most of us were given evacuation papers to cross the border. But somehow, when the evacuation papers came for my family, my name wasn't on the list. I was put on somebody else's evacuation papers. My name was included on a list from another family that we didn't even know. A decision was made to not say anything because, if we had said something about it, the authorities would probably have kept me in Poland.

On evacuation day, they put us on a train. It was a passenger train. It was just before Christmas—Christmas Eve. The train stopped shortly before the German border at the border crossing. The Russians were celebrating—either for Christmas or their imminent victory, or both. They were drinking heavily and drunk. Their drunkenness and lack of clarity helped us to cross the border with improper papers.

There were German trucks with supplies traveling over the border. When they realized what kind of mess we were in, they offered to help. We asked them if they would take us along. They said yes, but first, we had to bribe the Russian soldiers. Most people gave them money or alcohol. This is where we got separated from the other family who had my name on their evacuation papers. There was so much confusion, we jumped on any truck we could and met up later on the German side of the border in the immigration camp that was prepared for us. So, when I got into Germany, I didn't have any identification papers at all. I was so worried they were going to take me away from my aunt Amelia or send me back to Poland.

Because we had just come from a mismanaged immigration camp in Poland without proper resources, we were covered in lice. Everybody had lice. We were loaded with lice. It was so dirty in the Polish/Russian camp. So, the German camp staff stripped off all our clothes and threw them in the fire. They also cut off our hair. I had really long braids at that time, and they cut off all my hair. I must have been eleven or twelve years old. I remember it so clearly because it happened on Christmas day. Every Christmas, those memories re-emerge, and I think about my hair.

After Christmas, all the immigrants were redistributed to different villages with different placements. From that time forward, I could not be with my aunt Amelia anymore because I was an orphan without identification papers. My fears came true. I was placed in an orphanage.

Lutheran confirmation,
1948, Children's Home in East Germany

Lutheran confirmation

Orphanage/Children's Home, Hohen, Neuendorf, May 1948. I am top row, center.

Germany was being divided into four sectors, and I was placed in the Russian sector, East Germany. The orphanage was one train station out of Berlin. I was there for quite a while. This is where I went to school, but there was a problem with my schooling.

From the time we were forced to return to the farm in Poland by the Russians, including all the time we spent in different immigration camps during the formal evacuation of Poland, I had missed a whole year of school and was far behind academically. I had to do a lot of catching up. I also had to take a Russian class, and everyone, including me, had a crush on our handsome Russian teacher.

My friends at the Children's home in Hohen Neuendorf, Berlin, July 1950.

LIFE AFTER THE WAR

While at the orphanage, I was placed in the care of a foster family who owned a licensed pub. I lived there for several weeks but was returned to the orphanage because it was considered inappropriate for a child of my age to be in an environment where alcohol was being served and customers were drinking too much.

After I graduated from elementary school, I was placed in a foster home to help out a couple who fostered me briefly. They owned a local tavern.

Once I completed elementary school at the orphanage, I was expected to make my own living, so I had to attend a special school one day a week to learn to how to be a domestic in a household. During the rest of the week, I worked for a dentist's family in the French sector of Berlin.

(Berlin after the war was divided into 4 different occupation sectors: the French sector, the American sector, the British sector, and the Soviet sector.)

Working as a domestic for the dentist's wife in the French sector. On this day, we had an Easter egg hunt—1950.

It was during this period, while I was working with the dentist's family, that Julian was assigned to work for a farmer in Poland after he was taken from the Russian post war camp. He happened to be in the right place at the right time. A letter arrived at the post office, which was part of the farmer's house for whom he has been assigned. The letter was addressed to "Krueger or Stoltz". The postman, recognizing the name, brought it to Julian's attention, and Julian asked to see it. It was from Else who was trying to locate where her siblings were. She knew where I was, and Julian knew where Ali was. Julian hadn't seen me in seven years, and later said he wouldn't have recognized me if he walked past me on the street. It was a lucky coincidence. The letter found its way to Julian, which facilitated the reconnection of four of the family members.

Julia Kelm, my dad's youngest sister from Ontario, Canada, was also inquiring through her sister Bertha in Poland about where my dad's (Wilhelm's) children were. She and Aunt Schulberg, (living in Yorkton, Saskatchewan) were in contact. Aunt Schulberg agreed to be my sponsor in Canada and petitioned the Canadian government for permission to do so.

Accordingly, Julian sent me to Bremen Harbor, Germany, to complete the final procedures for immigration. I spent several weeks at the Canadian immigration camp helping out by working in the kitchen, eagerly waiting to hear if I would be sent to Canada.

Part of the immigration protocol was to have a completed medical examination. We discovered that I had a spot on my lung, which showed up in x-rays. I was not allowed to enter Canada until it could be determined that I did not have tuberculosis (TB).

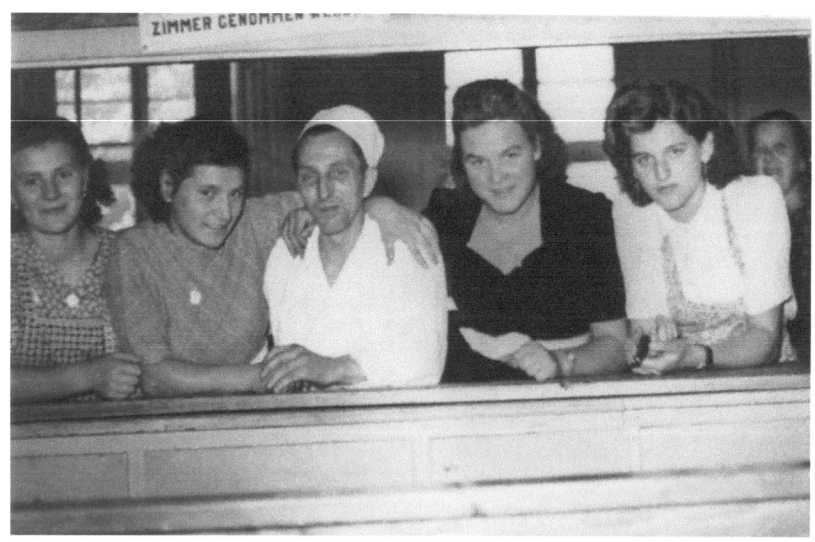

Me and my friends working in the kitchen at the Immigration camp in Bremen's Harbor, Germany. We are all waiting our turn for acceptance into Canada.

Karl Heinz and I worked together at the immigration camp in Bremen's Harbor. We were both sent out of the immigration camp for three months to wait for the results of our medical examinations, so I returned to the home of my sister Else in West Germany who lived with Aunt Hilda. Aunt Hilda wasn't my real aunt. She was a friend of Else's from the immigration camp, but we thought of her as an aunt.

Tragically, during this period, Karl Heinz was killed while working as a truck driver for a local business.

I was very anxious waiting for the medical results. It was difficult for me.

This is Karl Heinz, the first man I ever kissed.

Else married Harry Romeike. Here we are at their farm in Simmern, near Sargenroch. I am waiting for my medical results.

During these months, pending my immigration to Canada, I was chosen to go to a summer camp in Sauerland, Rotenburg on Zale, because I was an orphan and undernourished. But instead of getting healthier, I got really sick. I contracted yellow jaundice and was quarantined and put in a recovery room to convalesce. I was all alone, and I was so scared. Often there was lightning and thunder, and until this day, I still feel a little afraid of thunderstorms.

Guest House buildings (summer camp) at Sauerland, Rotenburg on Zale, 1950.

My medical examination showed that I did not have tuberculosis, and I was approved for immigration to Canada. I was eighteen years old when I left Germany, bound for St. John, New Brunswick, to be relocated in Yorkton, Saskatchewan. It was January of 1951. I was the first among my brother and sisters to come to Canada.

Left: Standing in front of the Bever-brae in Bremen's Harbor just before departure for St. John, Canada, September 20th, 1950. The crossing lasted 9 days.
Right: The text reads: "We're coming and going; there is no other way. If we see each other again, God alone will know. We discovered that through love, we stay connected over sea and over land."

Julian was the last one to leave Poland, and he ended up in West Germany as well. I don't know how Ali or Else fled Poland, but we learned much later that Irene was separated from the guardian family she was living with. We knew nothing of her whereabouts for seven years, or until she turned eighteen years old.

Else appealed to the Red Cross in 1952 to find Irene, who we had been missing for all those years. This is how we discovered that Irene had become separated from her foster family at the time of the formal evacuation from Poland. Eventually, she was found living in the home of a Catholic group helping refugees in Germany. She was then placed in a home for the disabled, where she was supposed to be properly educated. But Else was unhappy with what she saw and took guardianship of Irene because the home for the disabled was not teaching Irene anything, just giving her work to do. Whatever she learned, she learned from Else, including how to read and write.

When the war finally ended, the Soviets were conferred the Polish lands that encompassed our family farm, so it was repossessed by Soviet Poland.

The German government implemented an equalization program called *lústen auchgleich* and paid the original owners for the land only. Any money remaining in bank accounts was settled for only ten cents on the dollar (10%).

On board the Bever-brae. The coat I am wearing was a care package from my relatives in Chicago—Martha Kitzman and her brother Uncle Julius Stotz.

Else had to track down Julian, now in Canada, so he could apply for repayment before a deadline. The letter followed him to a number of places before it reached him, and fortunately the family was able to apply for repayment. The proceeds were eventually divided equally between the five siblings. Julian and I gave our share of the proceeds to Else, who was looking after Irene.

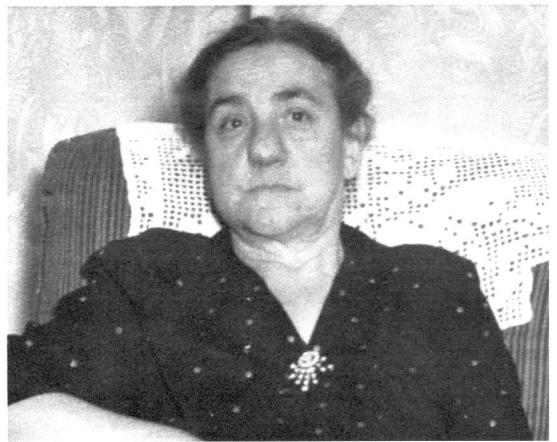

Martha Kitzman.

The Beaverbrae was used during WWII as a submarine maintenance vessel. It made 52 trans-Atlantic journeys to bring 33,000 refugees to Canada at the end of the war..

Beaverbrae ship5

LIVING IN CANADA

Upon arrival in Canada, our ship docked in St. John Harbor, and we spent the night in St. John, New Brunswick. We were all very worried about what would happen next. I really had no idea what to expect.

The next day, we boarded the Canadian Pacific Railway passenger train on route to Regina, Saskatchewan. My aunt Schulberg set everything up with the Canadian authorities. Everything was taken care of. I was even given a small amount of spending money, as we had to buy our own meals in the dining car. The money came from my aunt and uncle Schulberg, and I paid them back slowly over time for everything, including the cost for sponsorship.

We spent two days on the train. We slept in our seats with our identification badges around our necks. We had only one stop that allowed us to get off the train. That stop was Winnipeg, Manitoba. I do remember a Jewish shop where the owners spoke German. They made us feel at home, which was very comforting. At the end of the second day, we arrived in Regina, Saskatchewan.

I first lived with my aunt and uncle Schulberg on their farm in Yorkton for approximately one year. Canadian immigration required that I live on a farm for at least one year. I tried to be a helping hand on their neighbor's farm because the farm wife was pregnant and needed support, but it didn't work out. I was supposed to milk their cows, but I wasn't any good at it. I spoke almost no English and was worried about how I could get by.

The Schulberg farm in Yorkton, Saskatchewan. After I was married and had children, we used to visit Aunt and Uncle Schulberg on the farm. Both Erika and Rodney loved it here and have many fond memories.

Uncle Schulberg put me on my first horse.

While searching for a job, I heard of a family who were Swiss and spoke German. They ran a rooming house/restaurant nearby Qu'Appelle and were looking for domestic help, so I applied, and they gave me a job. I think their business is still running to the present day.

There was another girl working with me in Qu'Appelle who felt the owners were taking advantage of us. They made us work hard and paid us very little. She decided to quit and move to Regina. She said she had family in Regina who would help her out, and when she found a job there, I could be her roommate and work in Regina too. So, this is how and why I moved to Regina. She found me a job at the Regina General Hospital as kitchen staff on one of the upper floors.

Posing for a photo in front of a local bank in Yorkton

I lived in a rental house next to the hospital with a couple of girlfriends, and we all shared the rent. At one point, Ali roomed with me for a while. She was able to pay her own way over to Canada because she worked in Germany for a few years. This all happened before I was married.

Posing for a photo in front of the Regina General Hospital.

Before I was married, I lived alone in a small attic apartment on Albert street, but later, relocated to an apartment with some friends in a boarding house near the Hospital.

Rental house near Regina General Hospital.

Me with friends on the streets of Regina

I first met my husband, Karl (your grandfather), through a friend, Emil Presser. We were introduced at the Regina German-Harmonie Club, a large dance and assembly hall (bar included), which was very popular among the many German immigrants in Regina.

We dated for about a year and married on September 15th, 1953, when I turned twenty-one and no longer had to ask permission from my guardian, Aunt Schulberg. We had a small wedding at Grace Lutheran Church on Victoria Avenue, performed by a German pastor, because we knew very little English.

On a date with some friends and Karl.

The Regina German-Harmonie Club.

Karl and I after our engagement

Wedding Photo, September 15th, 1953

Wedding Photo, September 15th, 1953

Holding roses at my wedding, September 15, 1953

For our honeymoon, we boarded a Grey Hound bus in Regina, which stopped in Banff National Park for a one-day layover before continuing on to Vancouver and Victoria for about ten days. We typically stayed in inexpensive hotels—it's all we could afford.

Banff Spring Hotel in Banff National Park is a world-famous UNESCO Heritage Site.

Karl on the ski lift in Banff.

On board the BC Ferry traveling from Vancouver to Victoria

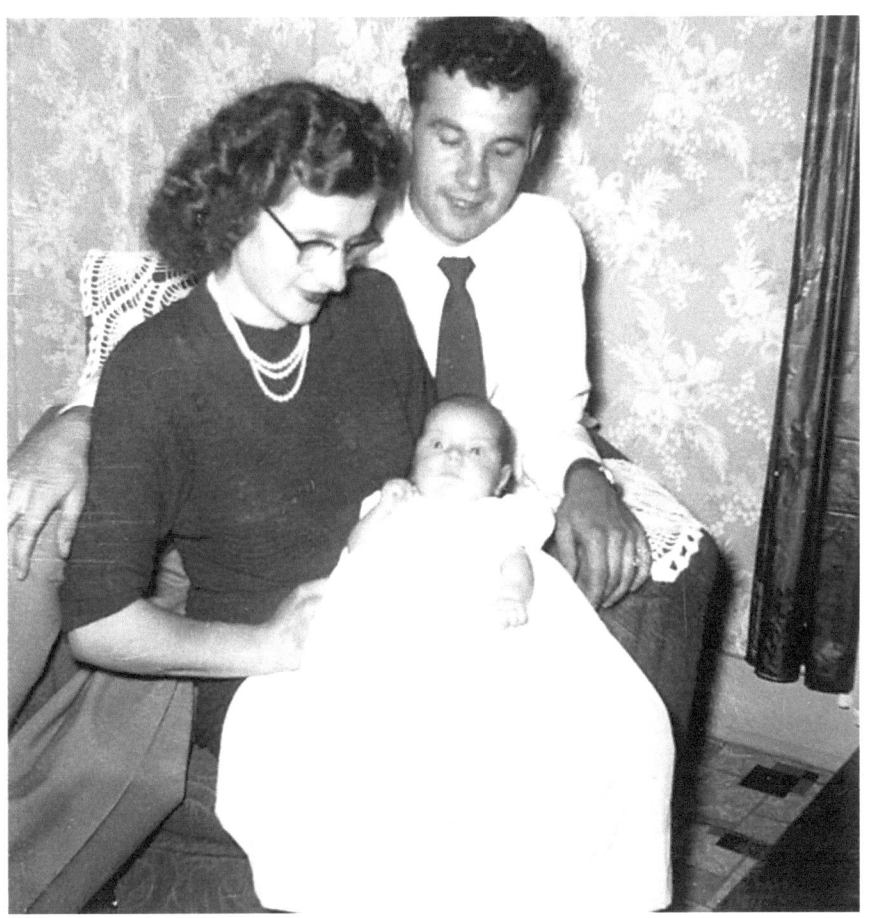

Surprise—Erika was a honeymoon baby and was born 9 months later

Dressed in the first suit I bought in Canada.

I continued working at the Regina General Hospital, but sadly, when the hospital supervisor discovered I was pregnant and had morning sickness, they asked me to quit my job. Fortunately, working at the Regina General Hospital forced me to learn quite a bit of English very quickly, and I soon found a job as a short-order cook at a Canadian Pacific Railway station. As a new couple, we really needed the money.

Before our marriage, Karl was living with his dad and his siblings on Mackay Street. After our marriage, for a very short time, I lived with Karl's relatives in a garage that was converted into a small bedroom suite. We did all our own cooking on a portable two-range electric cooktop.

There were 3 rooms in the house: a living room, kitchen, and one bedroom. There was a bed in each room to accommodate everyone. There was no running water; it had to be accessed at a nearby pump. The bathroom was an outhouse; that's why we had to bathe the children in the kitchen. It was a very humble beginning for us.

Baby Erika at Mackay Street, 11 months old

Baby Erika, 18 months old

Baby Rodney, 5 months old

Karl's father at McKay Street. It may be Elfriede sitting next to him.

Karl's father was admitted to the hospital with advanced lung cancer right after I returned home with our new baby, about a year after our wedding. He only saw baby Erika once before he died. The house was sold by a cousin, and I'm not sure where Karl's sisters, Wilma and Elfriede, ended up.

Karl's younger brother, Ed, lived with us for almost ten years. He was like an older brother to Erika and Rodney, who didn't know he was actually their uncle until their early teens.

Elfriede lived with Eduard and Wilma Koffler for a while but eventually ventured off to find her own way in the world. It must have been very difficult for Ed and Elfriede. They got uprooted a lot and must have felt they weren't wanted and were a burden on the family. Ed might be the only one who can clarify the living arrangements for him and his two sisters. Both Ed and Elfriede (brother and sister) are shown later in pictures at what I believe is King Street in Regina.

Me at our King Street duplex home—winter of 1955 or '56

For two years, I took care of both children while Karl worked as an electrician. When he returned home from work, I went to my part-time job as a service elevator operator at the Saskatchewan Hotel. At that time, all elevators required someone to operate them manually. Karl put the children to bed, but they didn't like it.

Ed, Erika, and Rodney at King Street. It was a duplex home, and Mrs. Cranfield was our neighbor and babysitter. Erika loved the doll she is cuddling. One day, she left it outside —on the front lawn—and someone took it.

Erika holding Rodney's favorite toy, a stuffed lassie dog.

Erika and Rodney at King Street during winter—1958/59

Christmas at King Street 1958/59.

We lived on King Street for 5 years and saved money for a new house. In 1960, we used my pension money from the Saskatchewan Hotel ($1,000.00) for a down payment and moved to 182 Hamilton Street North. In 1960, a new house on the North side of Regina cost $9,600.00 This is where my children spent most of their years growing up.

182 Hamilton Street North, where Rodney spent all of his elementary school years and Erika started in second grade. It was our first and only new family home in a new development.

I continued to work at the Saskatchewan Hotel for 39 years (mostly as a waitress in the Ranch Room—a Silver Service Restaurant) and retired early, at age 63.

The sixty years that followed, as wife, mother and grandmother, caring for my husband's health and caring for my children's future, are shared with you and your parents, Erika and Rodney, and their partners, Charlie and Nandini. They will remember the details much better than me, and I will let them tell their story, which is your story too.

Be sure to question them and be patient. The value of knowing your family background is yours to determine and hopefully cherish.

To the best of my recollection, this is the story of my early years. Like me, it is simple and direct. It was inspired by my daughter Erika, who worked hard to gather the details, and later prepared for publication by my son, Rodney. Many of the essential stories were contributed by my brother Julian, whose memories and experiences were broader than my own. Without them this memoir could not have been written.

I never intended this project to be a history lesson—just a collection of memories, feelings, challenges, circumstances, and inspirations that led me to Canada, where the family life we all share together began.

REMEMBER THIS

I want to pass a message along to my children, grandchildren, and hopefully great-grandchildren:

- Value others on their potential, not their history.
- Never give up. Always hold on to hope. Things will always get better if you do. Always.
- Despite the challenges of my life, I believe I was, and still am, very lucky. I have always felt this—that a guardian angel was watching over me every moment.

INDEX OF PHOTOGRAPHS

3-week Trans-Atlantic Ocean passage aboard the Bremen-Ubersee when I emigrated from Berlin to Canada in fall of 1950.

Community photo at my mother's funeral.

I think this is Christmas at Elliot Street with the Radmacher family and Elfriede

Uncle Julius with his wife.

Uncle Bruno Stolz.

Julia Kelm with son Walter on the right and an aunt's son Wille (cousin to me). Must be Bertha Fritz's son. This photo was probably taken in Windsor, Ontario

L–R: Walter Kelm, his mother (Julia), Aunt Bertha, and Adolph Fritz. Julia lives in Windsor, Ontario, and I believe Bertha is in Chicago. Not sure who's visiting who here. There's a K on the front door, so maybe the Fritzs are visiting the Kelms in Windsor

Martha Kitzman and her husband at their son Gilbert's wedding. She must have had a second son, as there are other photos with 2 daughters and another son

Else and Harry Romeike on their farm in Sargenroth.

Aunt Hilda on Else's farm in Sargenroth. Left to Right: Harry, Hilda, Angelika, and Else.

Erika and Rodney in the bunkhouse with Julian, Kamloops, 1963.

My sister Irene.

Aunt Schulberg and Uncle Schulberg 1954.

Summer camp at Sauerland, July 1950.

Summer camp at Sauerland, July 1950.

Ruth Schulberg and I in Yorkton, 1952.

My sister Ali.

Ruth Schulberg, 1952.

A friend and I at our rental house near the Regina General Hospital.

Edith and I on the farm in Yorkton.

Aunt Schulberg's son Norman, Victoria, BC.

Edith, Norman and me in Yorkton, Saskatchewan.

Else and Harry Romeike; Angelika and Maryanne, Harry's sister.

Me hugging a child in Yorkton.

Me and my roommate in Regina, Saskatchewan.

After my arrival in Canada, in Yorkton, 1951.

Me at the legislative building in Regina, Saskatchewan.

Wedding photo. Regina, Saskatchewan, 1953.

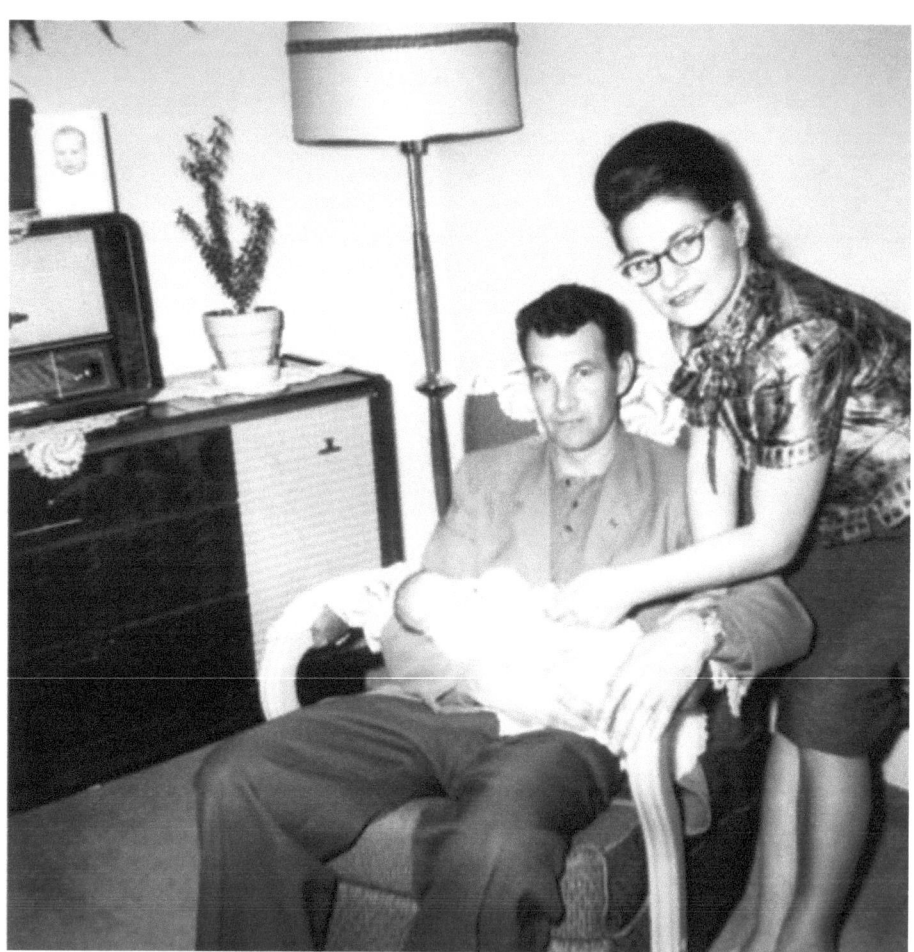

Me and Karl holding baby Mark Koffler, 1962. Note the fashion styles.

Me and Karl at our 10th Wedding anniversary, 1964.

Me and Karl on our 50th wedding anniversary 2003.

Me and Karl on our 40th wedding anniversary 1993.

FOOTNOTES

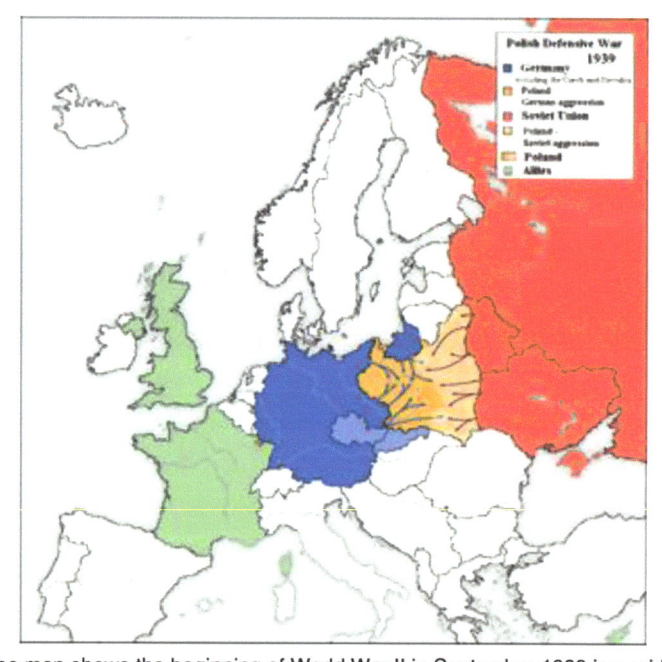

The map shows the beginning of World War II in September 1939 in a wider European context.

** The **1939 Soviet invasion of Poland** was a Soviet military operation that started without a formal declaration of war on 17 September 1939, during the early stages of World War II. Sixteen days after Nazi Germany invaded Poland from the west, the Soviet Union did so from the east. The invasion ended on 6 October 1939 with the division and annexing of the whole of the Second Polish Republic by Germany and the Soviet Union.

*** The Allied powers, who defeated Nazi Germany in World War II divided the country west of the Oder-Neisse line into four occupation zones for administrative purposes during 1945–1949. In the closing weeks of fighting in Europe, American forces had pushed beyond the previously agreed boundaries for the future zones of occupation, in some places by as much as 200 miles. The line of contact between Soviet and American forces at the end of hostilities was temporary. After two months in which they had held areas that had been assigned to the Soviet zone, American forces withdrew in the first days of July 1945. [1] Some have concluded that this was a crucial move that persuaded the Soviet Union to allow American, British, and French forces into their predesignated zones in Berlin, which occurred at roughly the same time (July 1945), although the need for intelligence gathering (see Operation Paperclip) may also have been a factor.

Szyszynskie Holendry - I and my siblings were all born here. (German spelling Schischinskie)

Laczki - Birthplace of my mother Berta Shrank

Sompolno - My parents were married here

Nowy Sacz - Birthplace of my paternal grandfather Gottleib Stoltz

Lesiska - My maternal grandmother Mathilde Wolter was born and died here

Pasieka - Birthplace of maternal great-great grandmother Karoline Benkendorf

Lipia Gora - Birthplace of my maternal great-great grandfather Michael Wolter

Osowiec - Michael Wolter died here

www.ingramcontent.com/pod-product-compliance
Lightning Source LLC
Chambersburg PA
CBHW040529020526

44117CB00027B/27